Prayers and Blessings
for the Morning

To...

Every morning offers a new beginning, a new blessing, a new hope.
May God bless you today.

From... Anne

Psalm 118:24
This is the day the LORD has made.
We will rejoice and be glad in it.
(New Living Translation)

D0248537

Lord,

I don't yet know what plans
you have for me today,
but I give each hour to you
praying that you will show me
how to use my time wisely and well.
Please bless my activities and endeavours today
so that, in turn, I can bless others
with your amazing love.
Amen.

Lord,

help me to remember that nothing is going
to happen to me today
that together you and I can't handle.

Anon

Psalm 5:3

Each morning you listen
to my prayer, as I bring my
requests to you and wait
for your reply.

(Contemporary English Version)

Judith Merrell, Whitby

3

All this day, O Lord
Let me touch
as many lives as possible for thee;
And every life I touch,
do thou by thy Spirit quicken,
Whether through the word I speak,
the prayer I breathe,
or the life I live.
Amen

Mary Sumner
Founder of the Mother's Union, 1828–1921

Ephesians 3:16

I pray that out of his glorious riches he may
strengthen you with power
through his Spirit in your inner being...

(New International Version)

Elizabeth Iliff, Flatford Mill

5

Lord,

Whatever I may say, I have it easy.
You know I've got problems –
you should, I spend most of my prayer time
telling you about them; and often, forgive me,
telling you exactly how I want them solved.
But when I look around with eyes and mind open
and see what others have to face
then I know - I have it easy.

There are folk around me with bigger problems than mine.
Frightened, anxious and lonely,
wanting a little bit of human contact.
Needing a little courage to face problems and hang on to life.
I can encourage them just by being with them, just by listening.
Just by taking off a bit of their load, like you take mine.
Is that what you want me to do?
I can't do it on my own – but thank you, Lord.
I don't have to.

Eddie Askew
Writer and Former International Director of The Leprosy Mission, 1927–2007
Extract from A Silence and A Shouting, *1982*

6

Phillippians 4:6–7
Don't worry
about anything;
instead, pray about
everything.
Tell God what you need,
and thank him for all
he has done.
Then you will experience
God's peace, which exceeds
anything we can understand.
His peace will guard
your hearts and minds
as you live in Christ Jesus.

(New Living Translation)

Brian Cartwright, Meerkat

7

When life is busy...

Lord, today is going to be a busy day.
I have so much to do and so little time.
Help me to discern what is important and what can be left.
Help me to prioritize and not feel pressurized.
Help me to lean on your strength today.

And Lord, help me to put aside the hurry and worry
simply to enjoy a few restoring moments with you.
Help me not to be so busy that I fail to see others' needs.
Help me to work at each task efficiently and with enjoyment
so that tonight, I will say that my day was rewarding and productive.

•

I have so much to do today
that I must set apart more time than usual to pray.

Martin Luther
German priest and reformer, 1483–1546

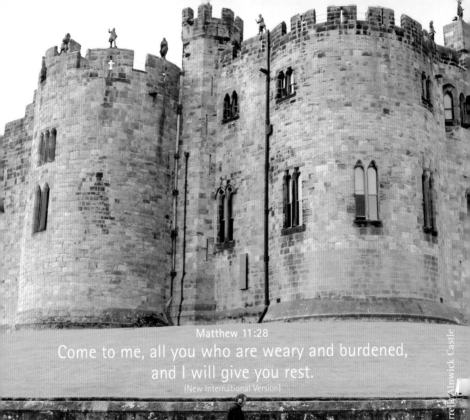

Matthew 11:28
Come to me, all you who are weary and burdened,
and I will give you rest.
(New International Version)

Judith Merrell/Alnwick Castle

9

Be Thou My Vision

Be thou my vision, O Lord of my heart,
Be all else but naught to me, save that thou art;
Thou my best thought in the day and the night,
Both waking and sleeping, thy presence my light.
Be thou my wisdom, be thou my true word,
Be thou ever with me, and I with thee Lord;
Be thou my great Father, and I thy true son;
Be thou in me dwelling, and I with thee one.
Be thou my breastplate, my sword for the fight;
Be thou my whole armour, be thou my true might;
Be thou my soul's shelter, be thou my strong tower:
O raise thou me heavenward, great Power of my power.
Riches I heed not, nor man's empty praise:
Be thou mine inheritance now and always;
Be thou and thou only the first in my heart;
O Sovereign of Heaven, my treasure thou art.
High King of Heaven, thou Heaven's bright sun,
O grant me its joys after victory is won.
Great heart of my own heart, whatever befall,
Still be thou my vision, O Ruler of all.

Eleanor Hull
Writer and journalist, 1860–1935
Original Irish words by Dallan Forgaill

I call to you, Lord,
at the dawn of this new day,
place into your hands
family and friends,
work to be done,
decisions I shall make,
obstacles I encounter,
strangers who pass my way,
the service I shall offer.

I call to you, Lord,
at the dawn of this new day,
my rock and my fortress,
my strength and my deliverer,
for all I am is yours,
each moment of this day
gifted to me by grace,
and offered in your name,
my offering of *praise*.

John Birch
Methodist local preacher and author

Charles Kinsey Duart Castle Isle of Mull

13

Sheila Adams, Lossiemouth Beach, Scotland

Old Sarum Prayer

God be in head and in my understanding;
God be in my eyes and in my looking;
God be in my mouth and in my speaking;
God be in my heart and in my thinking;
God be at my end and at my departing.

Sarum Primer, *1514*

Father God,

Thank you that I can give my worries
and concerns to you.
This evening, when I look back over my day,
I pray that I will be able to see
all the ways you have helped me.

Amen

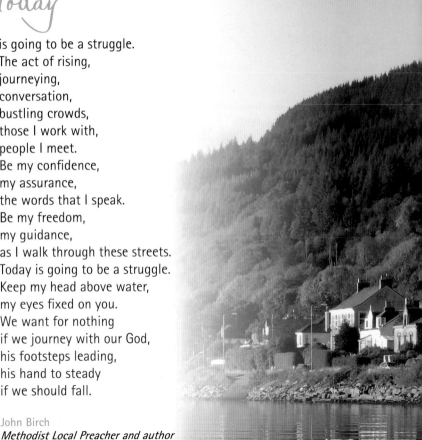

Today

is going to be a struggle.
The act of rising,
journeying,
conversation,
bustling crowds,
those I work with,
people I meet.
Be my confidence,
my assurance,
the words that I speak.
Be my freedom,
my guidance,
as I walk through these streets.
Today is going to be a struggle.
Keep my head above water,
my eyes fixed on you.
We want for nothing
if we journey with our God,
his footsteps leading,
his hand to steady
if we should fall.

John Birch
Methodist Local Preacher and author

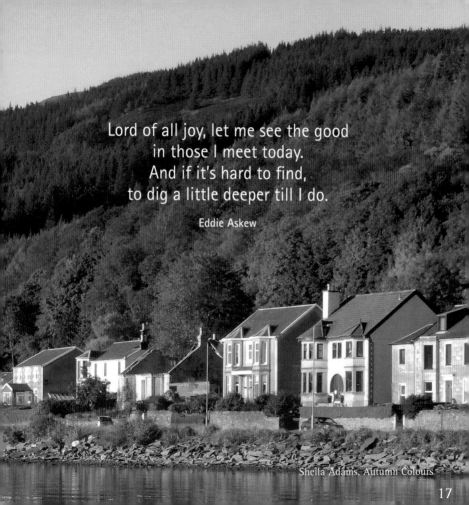

Lord of all joy, let me see the good
in those I meet today.
And if it's hard to find,
to dig a little deeper till I do.

Eddie Askew

Sheila Adams, Autumn Colours

17

Lord, open my eyes

that I may see you in creation power.
Open my heart,
that I may feel your love,
unblocking the arteries of life
to flow without constriction with life-giving warmth.
Open my mind, that I may know the glad certainty,
the daily celebration, of your presence.
Not just in nature's revelation,
but in your son.
One with you when life began,
and one with me as it goes on.
Open my lips,
that I may sing your praises
as I walk the road of faith, today.

Eddie Askew
Writer and Former International Director of The Leprosy Mission,
1927–2007

Psalm 115:15

May you be blessed by the LORD,
who made heaven and earth!

(Good News Translation)

Sheila Adams, Spring blossom

19

New Every Morning

Every day is a fresh beginning,
Listen my soul to the glad refrain.
And, spite of old sorrows
And older sinning,
Troubles forecasted
And possible pain,
Take heart with the day and begin again.

Susan Coolidge
American Children's writer,
author of What Katy Did, *1835–1905*

Lord, each new morning
is a special gift from you.

Thank you for the chance
to put past mistakes behind
and make a fresh start.

Thank you for the opportunity
to try again.

Help me to seize those moments
when I can offer a helping hand
or a listening ear.

Help me to make today a good day
for my family, my friends
and my community.

Be, Lord,

Within me to strengthen me,
Without me to guard me,
Over me to shelter me,
Beneath me to establish me,
Before me to guide me,
After me to forward me,
Round me to secure me.

Lancelot Andrewes
English Bishop, 1555–1626

22

Psalm 29:11

The LORD gives strength to his people; the LORD blesses his people with peace.

(New International Version)

Judith Merrell, Morning mist, Yorkshire

Traveller's Prayer

Alone with none but thee, my God,
I journey on my way.
What need I fear when thou art near,
Oh king of night and day?
More safe am I within thy hand
Than if a host did round me stand.

Saint Columba
Irish abbot and missionary, 521–597

Psalm 91:11
God will command his angels to
protect you wherever you go.
(Contemporary English Version)

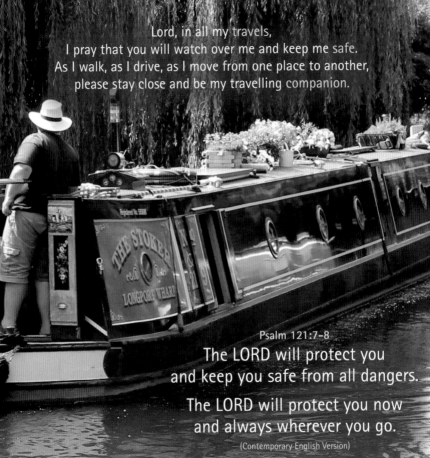

Lord, in all my travels,
I pray that you will watch over me and keep me safe.
As I walk, as I drive, as I move from one place to another,
please stay close and be my travelling companion.

Psalm 121:7-8
The LORD will protect you
and keep you safe from all dangers.

The LORD will protect you now
and always wherever you go.

(Contemporary English Version)

Lord Jesus,

Today
I give you my hands to do your work.
I give you my feet to go your way.
I give you my eyes to see as you do.
I give you my tongue to speak your words.
I give you my mind that you may think in me.
I give you my spirit that you may pray in me.
Above all, I give you my heart that you may love in me
your Father and all mankind.
I give you myself that you may grow in me,
so that it is you Lord Jesus,
who live and work and pray in me.

Anon
Used with Permission of The Grail

Ephesians 2:10

For we are God's handiwork,
created in Christ Jesus to do good works,
which God prepared in advance
for us to do.

(New International Version)

Judith Merrell. Purple heather, blue sky, Yorkshire

The light of God surrounds me
The love of God enfolds me
The power of God protects me
The presence of God watches over me.
Wherever I am, God is.

Anon

God hugs you.

You are encircled by the arms of
the mystery of God.

Saint Hildegard of Bingen
German Benedictine abbess, 1098–1179

Hebrews 13:5
For God has said, "I will never leave
you; I will never abandon you."

(Good News Translation)

29

You are a child of God

May today there be peace within.
May you trust God that you are exactly
where you are meant to be.
May you not forget the infinite possibilities
that are born of faith.
May you use those gifts that you have received,
and pass on the love that has been given to you.
May you be content knowing you are a child of God.
Let this presence settle into your bones,
and allow your soul the freedom to sing, dance,
praise and love.
It is there for each and every one of us.

Saint Teresa of Ávila
Spanish Carmelite nun, 1515–1582

God, give us grace to accept with *serenity*
the things that cannot be changed,
Courage to change the things which should be changed,
and the wisdom to distinguish the one from the other.

Living one day at a time,
Enjoying one moment at a time,
Accepting hardship as a pathway to peace.
Taking, as Jesus did,
This sinful world as it is,
Not as I would have it.
Trusting that You will make all things right,
If I surrender to Your will,
So that I may be reasonably happy in this life,
And supremely happy with You forever in the next.
Amen

Reinhold Niebuhr
American theologian, 1892–1971

Judith Merrell, Pathway through the Silver Birch

Numbers 6:24–26
'May the LORD bless you
and protect you.

'May the LORD smile on you
and be gracious to you.

'May the LORD show you his favour
and give you his peace.'

(New Living Translation)

Lord,
make me an instrument of thy peace.
Where there is hatred, let me sow love;
Where there is injury, pardon;
Where there is doubt, faith;
Where there is despair, hope;
Where there is darkness, light;
Where there is sadness, joy.

O divine Master, grant that I may not so much seek
To be consoled as to console,
To be understood as to understand,
To be loved as to love;
For it is in giving that we receive;
It is in pardoning that we are pardoned;
It is in dying to self that we are born to eternal life.

Saint Francis of Assisi
Italian Roman Catholic friar and preacher, 1182–1226

The things that we pray for, good Lord,
give us your grace to work for.

Sir Thomas More
English lawyer, author and Renaissance humanist.
1478–1535

Ray Price, Snowy landscene

Richard Ward, Abandoned rowing boat

38

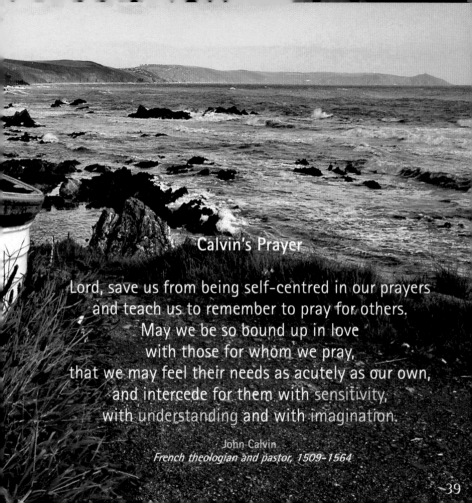

Calvin's Prayer

Lord, save us from being self-centred in our prayers
and teach us to remember to pray for others.
May we be so bound up in love
with those for whom we pray,
that we may feel their needs as acutely as our own,
and intercede for them with sensitivity,
with understanding and with imagination.

John Calvin
French theologian and pastor, 1509–1564

Take My Life

Take my life, and let it be
consecrated, Lord, to Thee.
Take my moments and my days;
let them flow in ceaseless praise.

Take my hands, and let them
move at the impulse of Thy love.
Take my feet, and let them be
swift and beautiful for Thee.

Take my voice, and let me sing
always, only, for my King.
Take my lips, and let them be
filled with messages from Thee.

Take my silver and my gold;
not a mite would I withhold.
Take my intellect, and use
every power as Thou shalt choose.

Take my will, and make it Thine;
it shall be no longer mine.
Take my heart, it is Thine own;
it shall be Thy royal throne.

Take my love, my Lord, I pour
at Thy feet its treasure store.
Take myself, and I will be
ever, only, all for Thee.

Frances Ridley Havergal
English poet and hymn writer, 1836–1879

An early morning paddle

1 Thessalonians 5:16–18

Rejoice always, pray
continually, give thanks in
all circumstances;

for this is God's will for you
in Christ Jesus.

(New International Version)

Charles Kinsey, Puffins with sand eels

42

Unclutter our lives, Lord,
we have too much,
consume too much,
expect too much.

Grant us perspective;
to see this world
through others' eyes
than just our own.

Grant us compassion;
where there is need
to play our part
not turn aside.

Grant us gratitude
for what we have,
our daily bread,
the gift of life.

Unclutter our lives, Lord,
give us space,
simplicity,
thankful hearts.

John Birch
Methodist Local Preacher and author

Thanks be to you,
our Lord Jesus Christ,
for all the benefits
which you have given us,
for all the pains and insults
which you have borne for us.